EGYPT'S LIBERATION

EGYPT'S LIBERATION

The Philosophy of the Revolution

PREMIER GAMAL ABDUL NASSER

Introduction by
Dorothy Thompson

Public Affairs Press, Washington, D. C.

INTRODUCTION

"These impressions of the philosophy of the revolution of July 23, 1952 were not meant to be published as a book . . . these thoughts are an effort to explore ourselves," says Premier Nasser in the preface to this short and in many ways remarkable book.

It is remarkable because it is an account of a revolution by a revolutionary leader who is conscious of the limitations of revolution—and of force.

It is remarkable for the absence of the Jacobin spirit which has undermined the spirit and institutions of the once revolutionary Liberal Democracies to the point where they tremble before the counter-revolutions that threaten the doom of order and liberty.

It is remarkable for the absence of personal egotism and power-lust so common to initiators of coups d'etat.

And it is remarkable for the painful, humble, self-searching and self-analysis that the leader of the Egyptian revolution makes of himself and — even more courageously — of his country and its people. In short, it is quite uniquely honest.

This book is not the work of a propagandist or "public relations expert," who might well, indeed, have advised against publishing anything so candid. Their operational field is not to promote candor but to suppress it. The enemies of Egypt (and of the Arab world) will almost certainly seize upon Premier Nasser's account of his disillusionment with the immediate aftermath of the overthrow of the old regime — a disillusionment with the national forces that the Junta of young officers expected to rally in unity, and of which they conceived themselves to be only a vanguard, prepared to yield place to older and wiser men.

His description of how they actually behaved, leaders of opinion and masses alike, is a bitter indictment. Abdul Nasser was looking for constructive ideas, for men ready to subject their personal ambitions, interests, and hatreds to a concentrated and consecrated effort for the renaissance of the nation.

"We needed order but we found nothing behind us but chaos. We needed unity . . . we found dissension. We needed work . . . we found indolence and sloth. . . . Every man we questioned had nothing to recommend except to kill someone else. Every idea we listened to was nothing but an attack on some other idea. If we had gone along with everything we heard we would have killed off all the people and torn down every idea, and there would have been nothing to do but sit down among the corpses and ruins. . . .

"We were deluged with petitions and complaints . . . but most of these cases were no more or less than demands for revenge, as though a revolution had taken place in order to become a weapon in the hand of hatred and vindictiveness."

I can hear voices saying (with vindictive satisfaction) "That's the Egyptians for you!"

To this we say that every revolution at

once social and national with whose record we are familiar has let loose similar terrible forces. But their leaders have not sought to restrain these forces but rather to inflame and exacerbate them, and by setting each against all mount to the absolute power to suppress each and all.

Abdul Nasser reveals himself as a patriotic idealist animated, initially, by too naive a faith in his people. But revolutions do not occur if the political body is sound, or if there is, in fact, and functioning, what Walter Lippmann has called a "public philosophy." The aftermath of the Egyptian revolution has only been proof of its inevitability and necessity. The illness which caused it could not, as he soon saw, be cured merely by sweeping away King, Court, and a ruling oligarchy. Centuries of experiences, myriads of factors, had contributed to the national character he is intent upon reforming.

Interesting, and I think truthfully revealing, is his analysis of the effect of Mameluke rule, through many dark centuries, on the Egyptian character. National characters are neither formed nor reformed in a day. The task of the transformer is beyond the lifetime of any single man, and the weak, seeking to guide a simultaneous national and social revolution will quickly abandon it in disillusionment. But Abdul Nasser is not weak because he is not blood-thirsty. He appears in these pages as one who can draw a new breath and gain new insights out of initial disillusionment; who out "of wounds and sore defeats" can make his "battlestay."

The struggle is never over. But he who can master corruption without being corrupted, can wield power without installing tyranny, and can master events without losing his own soul is a hero in history.

So far this man remains pure. Pure, faithful, and brave.

In Islamic theology, God is endowed with 99 attributes. Abdul, or Abd-el, means "servant of," and the rest of the name expresses one of these attributes — unless it is Abdullah, which means, direct-

ly, "servant of Allah" — of God. Thus
Abd-el Kerim means servant of the Gen-
erous One; Abd-el Mon'im, servant of the
Gentle One.

Abdul Nasser means servant of the Victorious One: Servant of God victorious.

May it be so.

DOROTHY THOMPSON

PREFACE

These impressions on the philosophy of the revolution of July 23, 1952, were not meant to be published as a book. Nor are they an attempt to explain the objectives and events of the revolution. They are put down for an entirely different purpose.

Like a reconnaissance patrol, these thoughts are an effort to explore within ourselves — to discover who we are and what our role is to be in the succeeding stages of Egypt's history.

They are an attempt to explore the path of the future, which must lead us through those conditions of the past and present with which we are now surrounded.

They are an effort to formulate our objectives and to measure the resources which must be mobilized to achieve them.

These thoughts seek to discover the pattern of our national environment and to make clear that we do not exist as an isolated island surrounded by troubled waters.

Such is my purpose: a reconnaissance patrol in the field on which we are fighting our greatest battle — for the complete liberation of our country.

GAMAL ABDUL NASSER

CONTENTS

INTRODUCTION—*Dorothy Thompson* 9

PREFACE 11

PART ONE 15

PART TWO 47

PART THREE 79

NOTES ABOUT THE AUTHOR 115

PART ONE

Elementary school student. The ultimate roots. Whence the revolution? Egypt was the center of our dreams. A great Faluja. Even the enemy. Before February 4. And before 1935. Truth . . . and vacuum. Aspirations and measures. The role of vanguard. Symbol of the revolution. Weapon in the hand of hate. Evils of egotism. Duties and responsibilities. The complete picture. Between the millstones. Only the army. On two roads at once. The will of fate.

15

First, I should like to dwell for a moment on the word "philosophy". It is a big word. As I contemplate it, I feel that I stand before a boundless world, a bottomless sea — and a trepidation restrains me from plunging into it since, from my point of vantage, I see no other shore to head for.

The truth is, I want to avoid the word "philosophy" in what I am about to say. Besides, it is difficult to discuss the philosophy of the Egyptian revolution — difficult for two reasons. In the first place, an exposition of the philosophy of the revolution of 1952 would require the thorough investigation by scholars into its roots, which strike so deeply into the history of our people. The story of national struggle contains no gaps filled with nothingness; neither does it feature any surprises that leap into existence without introduction. The struggle of any people, generation after generation, is a structure rising stone upon stone. And just as each stone finds firm support in the stone beneath it so, too,

17

do the episodes in the struggles of a people support each other. Each new event stems from the one preceding, and each becomes in turn the basis for a new one to follow.

Elementary School Student

I do not want to claim for myself the role of a history professor; nothing could be further from my mind. But were any elementary school student to attempt a study of the struggles of our people, he would discover that the revolution of July 23rd marks the realization of the hope held by the people of Egypt since they began, in modern times, to think of self-government and complete sovereignty.

There was an unsuccessful attempt to realize this hope when Sayyid Omar Makram led the movement to install Muhammed Ali ruler of Egypt in the name of its people. Another attempt failed when Arabi tried to secure a constitution. Many other attempts that also ended in grief were made during the period of intellectual ferment between the Arabi revolution and the

1919 revolution. This 1919 revolution, which was led by Sa'ad Zaghlul, was no more successful than the others in fulfilling the hopes of the people.

The Ultimate Roots

It is not true that the successful revolution of 1952 stemmed from what happened in the Palestinian War; nor is it true that it was due to the defective weapons which caused the death of our men and officers. Still further from the truth are statements that the cause lay in the electoral crisis in the Army Officers Club in 1951.

In my view, the real cause must be sought further and is more profound. Had the Army officers attempted the revolt in their own account because they were inveigled into the Palestine War, or because they had been shocked by the defective weapons scandal, or because of the attack on their honor in the club elections, it could not have been called a revolution — mutiny would have been a more appropriate name.

These were only incidental causes. Perhaps their greatest influence was to give us added impetus to going ahead with our plans for the revolution, although we had already embarked on this course for other reasons.

Whence the Revolution?

Let me now try, after all that has happened and after the long years that have gone by since the idea of revolt began to take root, to go back in my memory to the first day I discovered within myself the seeds of this idea.

The seeds were planted long before those days of November 1951, when the crisis in the Army Officers Club began. For by that time the Free Officers' organization was in existence and active. In fact, it is no exaggeration to say that the election crisis in the club was chiefly due to the activity of the Free Officers, for we intended at that time to enter the battle to test our strength of solidarity and organization.

The day we conceived that idea was also long before the scandal of defective weapons broke upon us. The Free Officers were already in existence, and it was in fact their pamphlets which first sounded the alarm. Their activity inspired the uproar which followed the scandal.

Egypt Was the Center of Our Dreams

No, the idea started long before that. It was further back even than May 16, 1948, the day which marked the beginning of my involvement in the Palestine War.

When I now try to recall the details of our experience in Palestine, I find a curious thing: we were fighting in Palestine, but our dreams were centered in Egypt. Our bullets were aimed at the enemy in his trenches before us, but our hearts hovered over our distant country, which we had left to the care of the wolves.

In Palestine, Free Officer cells found opportunity to study and investigate and to meet in the trenches and command posts. Salah Salem and Zakaria Muhyi ed-

21

Din came to me in Palestine after breaking through the siege lines into Faluja. We sat there in our besieged positions, not knowing what the outcome would be, but our conversation dwelt only upon our country, which it was our soldiers' duty to defend.

One day, Kamal ed-Din Hussein was sitting near me in Palestine, looking distracted, with nervous, darting eyes. "Do you know what Ahmed Abdul Aziz said to me before he was killed?" he said.

"What did he say?" I asked.

He replied with a sob in his voice and a deep look in his eyes, "He said to me, 'Listen, Kamal, the biggest battlefield is in Egypt.'"

A Greater Faluja

Not only did I meet in Palestine the friends who collaborated with me in the work for the sake of Egypt, but I encountered there also the ideas which illuminated the path ahead of me. I recall a time when I was sitting in the trenches thinking of our problems. Faluja was surrounded, and the enemy was subjecting it to a terrific air and artillery bombardment. I used often to say to myself: Here we are in these foxholes, surrounded, and thrust treacherously into a battle for which we were not ready, our lives the playthings of greed, conspiracy and lust, which have left us here weaponless under fire.

And when I would come to this point in my thinking, I used to find my thoughts suddenly leaping across the field and over the borders into Egypt, and I would say to myself: Over there is our country, another Faluja on a larger scale. What is happening to us here is a picture in miniature of what is happening to Egypt. Egypt too is besieged by difficulties and enemies; *she* has been deceived and forced into a battle for which *she* was not ready, *her* fate the toy of greed, conspiracy and lust, which left *her* without weapons under fire.

Even the Enemy

In addition to the companions who dis-

cussed with me in Palestine the future of
our country, and the experience which
hammered out our ideas as to the possibilities of its fate, the enemy, too, played
a role in reminding us of our country and
its problems. A few months ago, I read
some articles written about me by an
Israeli officer named Yeruhan Cohen,
which appeared in the *Jewish Observer*.
In these articles the Jewish officer relates
how he met me during the armistice ne-
gotiations.

"The subject which Gamal Abdul Nasser
always talked about with me," he wrote,
"was the struggle of Israel against the English, and how we organized the under-
ground resistance movement against them
in Palestine, and how we were able to
muster world public opinion behind us in
our struggle against them."

Before February 4th

The seeds of the revolution were present
within me long before the episode of February 4, 1942, a day after which I wrote

to a friend, saying, "What is to be done now that the die was cast and we accepted what happened on our knees in surrender? As a matter of fact, I believe the Imperialist was playing with only one card in his hand, with the object of threatening us. But once the Imperialist realizes that some Egyptians are ready to shed their own blood and meet force with force, he will beat a hasty retreat, like any harlot rebuffed."

Such, of course, is the usual practice of Imperialism. As for us, as for the Army, the episode had a new electrifying effect on our spirit and sensibilities. Heretofore officers who had talked only of selfish amusement now began to talk of self-sacrifice and their readiness to die in defense of their honor. They all voiced their regret for not having intervened, despite their obvious weakness, to restore to their country its honor and cleanse it with their own blood.

But for him who waits, tomorrow is close.

Some indeed tried to do something afterwards by way of retaliation, but the opportunity was irretrievably lost, leaving our hearts full of bitter anger and sorrow. Actually this action (on the part of the Imperialist), or rather this stab, revived the spirit of some of us and brought home to us the fact that when our honor was involved we might be prepared to defend it. It was a lesson, but it was a hard lesson.

And Before 1935

The day of my awakening was even earlier than that explosive period when, as a student, I marched in 1935 with the demonstrators who clamored for the restoration of the 1923 Constitution (which was actually restored), and when I was going around with delegations of students to the homes of Egyptian leaders in an attempt to get them to unite in behalf of Egypt. The National Front was formed in 1936 as a result of those efforts.

I recall that during that period of ferment, I wrote a letter to one of my friends. It was dated September 2, 1935.

26

"Dear Brother,

"I talked to your father on the telephone on the 30th, asking after you. He told me that you were at school. So I decided to put down in writing what I intended to communicate to you on the telephone. Allah said 'Oppose them with whatever forces you can muster.' But where are these forces we are supposed to have in readiness for them? The situation today is precarious, and Egypt's situation is even worse. We are on the verge of collapse and death, for truly the temple of despair has mighty columns. But, who is to pull it down?" I continued my letter in this vein.

When was the day on which I discovered the seeds of revolution within me? The truth is that these seeds were not only hidden in me; I found them also in the hearts of a great many others, who in turn could not pinpoint the beginnings of their existence. Is it not clear then that these seeds were implanted in us when we were born, and that they were a hope concealed

27

in our subconsciousness, put there by the generation before us?

Truth . . . and Vacuum

I have made this long digression in order to describe the primary reason for the difficulty confronting me in speaking of the philosophy of the revolution because such a discussion requires the deep research of scholars into the historical origins of our people.

The second reason is that I myself was inside the maelstrom of the revolution, and from those who find themselves in a maelstrom, some of its more distant details are hidden. I was heart and soul involved in everything that happened and the way it happened; how, then, can I deal with it objectively, or with the hidden significance behind it?

I am one of those who believe that nothing can exist in a vacuum; even truth cannot so exist. Truth is that which we feel and know in our hearts to be right, or to be more exact, that which our souls embrace. Our souls are the vessels in which everything we are is contained; and everything we are, everything placed in these vessels, must take their shape, even truth. I try as much as humanly possible to prevent my soul from altering the shape of truth very much, but how far can I succeed? That is the question.

Beyond this, I want to be fair to myself and fair to the philosophy of the revolution. So I leave it to history to draw up its outlines as I see them, as others see them, and as they are demonstrated by events — and then to distill from all this the full truth.

Aspirations and Measures

What, then, can I say? I am qualified to talk of two things. The first is embraced in the term "aspirations", which began in the form of a vague hope, then developed into a defined idea, and finally into a practical program at midnight July 23rd.

The second is the measures we have taken to put these aspirations, with all their vague hopes, their defined ideas and their

29

practical programs, into practical execution since midnight July 23rd up to now.

It is about these aspirations and measures that I wish to speak.

For a long time I have been asking myself: Was it necessary for us, the Army, to do what we did on July 23, 1952?

I have already observed that the revolution marked the realization of a great hope felt by the people of Egypt since they began, in modern times, to think in terms of self-government and to demand that they have the final word in determining their own future. But if that is so, and if what happened on July 23rd was neither a military mutiny nor a popular uprising, why then was it entrusted to the Army, and not to other forces, to bring it about?

I have always been a confirmed believer in the ideal of the military service. It imposes one duty on the Army: that it should die on the frontiers of the motherland. Why did our Army find itself obliged to act in the capital of the motherland instead of on the frontiers?

30

Again, let me draw your attention to the fact that the rout in Palestine, and the defective arms, and the crisis in the Officers' Club were not the real sources from which poured out the torrent: all these were only contributory factors to the speed of the flow; but, as I said before, they were never the real origin.

But why the Army? I have long asked myself this question; I asked it during the stages of hope, thinking and planning prior to July 23rd, and I have continued to ask it during the many stages of action since then.

There were various justifications before July 23rd which made it clear to us why it was necessary for us to do what we did. We used to say, "If the Army does not do this job, who will?" We also used to say, "We have been used by the Despot as a bogey to give the people nightmares; now it is high time that the bogey be turned against the Despot to shatter his own dreams." We said many other things, but we felt to the depth of our beings this was

31

our soldiers' duty and that if we failed to discharge it, we would be failing in the sacred trust placed in us.

I confess, however, that the full picture did not become clear in my mind until after a long period of trial after July 23rd. It was the details of this experience which filled in the details of the picture.

The Role of Vanguard

I can testify that there were certain critical occasions since July 23rd when I accused myself, my comrades and the rest of the Army, of stupidity and madness for doing what we had done on that day.

Before July 23rd, I had imagined that the whole nation was ready and prepared, waiting for nothing but a vanguard to lead the charge against the battlements, whereupon it would fall in behind in serried ranks, ready for the sacred advance towards the great objective. And I had imagined that our role was to be this commando vanguard. I thought that this role would never take more than a few hours.

Then immediately would come the sacred advance behind us of the serried ranks and the thunder of marching feet as the ordered advance proceeded towards the great objective. I heard all this in my imagination, but by sheer faith it seemed real and not the figment of imagination.

Then suddenly came reality after July 23rd. The vanguard performed its task and charged the battlements of tyranny. It threw out Farouk and then paused, waiting for the serried ranks to come up in their sacred advance toward the great objective.

Symbol of the Revolution

For a long time it waited. Crowds did eventually come, and they came in endless droves — but how different is the reality from the dream! The masses that came were disunited, divided groups of stragglers. The sacred advance toward the great objective was stalled, and the picture that emerged on that day looked dark and ominous; it boded danger. At this moment

I felt, with sorrow and bitterness, that the task of the vanguard, far from being completed, had only begun.

We needed order, but we found nothing behind us but chaos. We needed unity, but we found nothing behind us but dissension. We needed work, but we found behind us only indolence and sloth. It was from these facts, and no others, that the revolution coined its slogan.

Weapon in the Hand of Hate

We were not yet ready. So we set about seeking the views of leaders of opinion and the experience of those who were experienced. Unfortunately we were not able to obtain very much.

Every man we questioned had nothing to recommend except to kill someone else. Every idea we listened to was nothing but an attack on some other idea. If we had gone along with everything we heard, we would have killed off all the people and torn down every idea, and there would have been nothing left for us to do but sit

34

down among the corpses and ruins, bewailing our evil fortune and cursing our wretched fate.

We were deluged with petitions and complaints by the thousands and hundreds of thousands, and had these complaints and petitions dealt with cases demanding justice or grievances calling for redress, this motive would have been understandable and logical. But most of the cases referred to us were no more or less than demands for revenge, as though the revolution had taken place in order to become a weapon in the hand of hatred and vindictiveness.

The Evils of Egotism

If anyone had asked me in those days what I wanted most, I would have answered promptly: To hear an Egyptian speak fairly about another Egyptian. To sense that an Egyptian has opened his heart to pardon, forgiveness and love for his Egyptian brethren. To find an Egyptian who does not devote his time to tearing down the views of another Egyptian.

In addition to all this, there was a confirmed individual egotism. The word "I" was on every tongue. It was the solution to every difficulty, the cure for every ill. I had many times met eminent men — or so they were called by the press — of every political tendency and color, but when I would ask any of them about a problem in the hope he could supply a solution, I would never hear anything but "I".

Economic problems? He alone could understand them; as for the others, their knowledge on the subject was that of a crawling infant. Political issues? He alone was expert. No one else had gotten beyond the a-b-c's of politics. After meeting one of these people, I would go back in sorrow to my comrades and say, "It is no use. If I had asked this fellow about the fishing problems in the Hawaiian Islands, his only answer would be 'I'."

Duties and Responsibilities

I remember visiting once one of our uni-

versities where I called the professors together and sat with them in order to benefit from their scholastic experience. Many
of them spoke before me and at great
length. It was unfortunate that none of
them advanced any ideas; instead, each
confined himself to advancing himself to
me, pointing out his unique fitness for making miracles. Each of them kept glancing
at me with the look of one who preferred
me to all the treasures of earth and heaven.

I recall that I could not restrain myself,
so I stood up and said, "Every one of us is
able in his own way to perform a miracle.
His primary duty is to bend every effort to
his work. And if you, as university professors, were to think of your students'
welfare, and consider them as you should,
your basic work, you would be in a position to provide us with the fundamental
strength to build up our motherland.

"Everyone must remain at his post, to
which he should dedicate all his efforts.
Do not look at us — we have been forced
by circumstances to leave our posts in

order to perform a sacred duty. If the motherland had no need for us other than to stay in the ranks of the Army as professional soldiers, we would have remained there."

What I did not say at that time was to give them the example of the members of the Revolution Council. I did not want to tell the professors that, before they were called to a greater duty, these men had been devoting all their energies to their jobs. I did not point out to them that most of the Revolution Council were professors at the General Staff College, and that this constituted a proof as to their distinction in their field as professional soldiers.

Likewise, I refrained from pointing out that three of the Revolution Council, Abdul Hakim Amer, Salah Salem and Kemal ed-Din Hussein, were given exceptional promotions on the field of battle in Palestine. I did not want to mention all this, because I do not want to boast about members of the Revolution Council, they being my brothers and comrades.

The Complete Picture

I confess that this whole situation produced in me a psychological crisis; but the events that followed, and my reflections thereon, together with the real meaning I could adduce from them, tended to ease my distress and set me to seek a justification for this situation, which I found when the whole picture of the motherland's plight rose somewhat clearly before my eyes. This clarification, moreover, brought me the answer to the question which had long bothered me, namely: Was it necessary for us, the Army, to do what we did on July 23rd?

The answer is yes, beyond any subterfuge or equivocation. I can say now that we did not ourselves define the role given us to play; it was the history of our country which cast us in that role.

I can now state that we are going through two revolutions, not one revolution. Every people on earth goes through two revolutions: a political revolution by which it wrests the right to govern itself

39

from the hand of tyranny, or from the army
stationed upon its soil against its will; and
a social revolution, involving the conflict
of classes, which settles down when justice
is secured for the citizens of the united
nation.

Peoples preceding us on the path of human progress have passed through two
revolutions, but they have not had to face
both simultaneously; their revolutions, in
fact, were centuries apart in time. For us,
the terrible experience through which our
people are going is that we are having both
revolutions at the same time.

Between the Millstones

This terrible experience stems from the
fact that both revolutions have attendant
factors which clash and contradict vio-
lently. To be successful, the political revolution must unite all elements of the nation, build them solidly together and instill
in them the spirit of self-sacrifice for the
sake of the whole country. But one of the
primary features of social revolution is that

it shakes values and loosens principles, and sets the citizenry, as individuals and classes, to fighting each other. It gives free rein to corruption, doubt, hatred and egoism.

We are caught between the millstones of the two revolutions we are fated now to be going through. One revolution makes it obligatory that we unite and love one another, fighting side by side to achieve our ends; the other brings dissension upon us against our desires, causing us to hate each other and think only of ourselves.

Between these two millstones, for example, the 1919 revolution was lost; it was unable to make secure the results it should have achieved. The ranks which formed in 1919 and faced up to tyranny were soon scattered by the outbreak of strife and conflict between individuals and classes. The result was dismal failure. Tyranny tightened its grip afterwards, overtly by means of occupation troops, and covertly through its masked stooges led by Sultan Fuad and King Farouk after him. The people harvested nothing except self-doubt, evil, hatred and rancour between individuals and classes.

Only the Army

The hope reposed in the 1919 revolution was thus dimmed. I say dimmed, but not extinguished, because the natural forces of resistance called into being by the great aspirations of our people did not cease to be active and to prepare for a new attempt.

This was the state of affairs which existed after the 1919 revolution, and which singled out the Army as the force to do the job. The situation demanded the existence of a force set in one cohesive framework, far removed from the conflict between individuals and classes, and drawn from the heart of the people: a force composed of men able to trust each other; a force with enough material strength at its disposal to guarantee a swift and decisive action.

These conditions could be met only by the Army.

In this way, as I have already remarked, it was not the Army which defined its role in the events that took place; the opposite is closer to the truth. The events and their ramifications defined the role of the Army in the great struggle to free the nation.

I have been aware since the beginning that our unity is dependent upon our full realization of the nature of circumstances in which we found ourselves, the historical circumstances of our country. For we could not alter the circumstances by the mere stroke of a pen, nor could we turn back the hands of the clock, or advance them — we could not control time. It was not within our power to stand on the road of history like a traffic policeman and hold up the passage of one revolution until the other had passed by in order to prevent a collision. The only thing possible to do was to act as best we could and try to avoid being ground between the millstones.

It was inevitable that we go through the

two revolutions at the same time. When we moved along the path of the political revolution and dethroned Farouk, we took a similar step on the path of the social revolution by deciding to limit land ownership.

I continue to believe that the July 23rd revolution must maintain its initiative and ability to move swiftly in order to perform the miracle of traveling through two revolutions at the same time, however contradictory our resulting actions might at times appear.

When one of my comrades came to me saying, "You want unity to face the English, but at the same time you allow the treason courts to continue their work," I listened to him with our great crisis in mind, the crisis of the millstones — a revolution on the one hand which obliges us to unite in one phalanx and to forget the past, and on the other hand, another revolution which demands that we restore lost dignity to our moral values by not forgetting the past. I might have replied that our only salvation lies, as I said before, in maintaining our speed of movement and our initiative, and our ability to travel through two revolutions simultaneously.

This situation does not exist because I wished it, or because all those who participated in the revolution have wished it. It is brought about by the act of fate, the history of our people, and the stage it is passing through at the present time.

PART TWO

What is it? Bullets talk. One had to go. Cries pursued me. Thoughts in the night. The search for an "Action". A single step. Residue of the past. Driven by storms. A society that is crystallizing. Well then, what is the path? This is our role. The past and the future.

But what is it we want to do? And how is it to be done?

The truth is I have often known the answers to the first question, and I am sure I was not the only one, for it was the hope and dream of our entire generation. As for the second question—the way to achieve what we want—I admit that this has undergone more change than anything else in my thinking. Also, in my opinion, it is the subject on which we are now most divided.

There can be no doubt that all of us dream of an Egypt free and strong. That is something about which there is no dispute between one Egyptian and another. But as for the way to achieve freedom and strength, that is our Gordian knot.

I came up against this problem before July 23rd, 1952, and it has continued to dominate my thoughts ever since. As a result, many of the aspects caught in the shadows have become clear, and horizons obscured by the darkness which for cen-

turies shrouded our country began to re-
solve themselves before my eyes. As my
thinking progressed, I began to realize the
great necessity for a "positive action."

What Is It?

But *what* action? To write the words
"positive action" on a piece of paper is a
simple matter. But in real life, and under
conditions besetting our generation, and in
face of the ordeals which, like vultures,
have dug their talons into the life of our
country, this is not enough.

For a brief period, positive action in my
estimation meant my own enthusiasm and
zeal. But this idea changed, and I began
to see that it was not enough for me to
merely be enthusiastic; I had also to in-
spire others to enthusiasm.

In those earlier days, I led demonstra-
tions in the Nahda Secondary School, and
I shouted from my heart for complete in-
dependence, and many others behind me
shouted, too. But our shouts only raised
dust which was blown by the wind, and

produced only weak echoes which shook no mountains and shattered no rocks.

Then I began to think that this positive action would be to demand that the leaders of Egypt unite to agree upon a single policy; so we went around in groups, shouting and excited, to visit their houses, demanding in the name of Egyptian youth that they agree on a single policy. But their agreement, when it came, dealt a severe blow to my expectations. The policy upon which they decided was the Treaty of 1936.

Bullets Talk

The second World War and the short period before it fired the spirit of our youth, and moved our whole generation towards violence. I confess — and I trust the Public Prosecutor will not take me to task — that to my excited imagination at that time political assassinations appeared to be the positive action we had to adopt if we were to rescue the future of our country. I considered the assassination of many

individuals, having decided that they were
the main obstacles which lay between our
beloved country and its destined greatness.
I began to study their crimes and to take it
upon myself to judge the harmfulness of
their actions.

I even considered the assassination of
the ex-king and some of his entourage who
had such utter disregard for the things we
held sacred. And I was not alone in thinking thus. When I had occasion to be with
others, we went beyond mere thinking to
planning. So many were the projects I
made in those days and so many were the
sleepless nights spent in preparing this
long-awaited positive action!

Our life during that period was like a
thrilling detective story. We had dark
secrets and passwords. We lurked in the
shadows; we had caches of pistols and
hand-grenades, and firing bullets was our
cherished hope. We made many attempts
in this direction, and I can still remember
our emotions and feelings as we dashed
along that melodramatic path to its end.

One Had To Go

Deep in my heart, however, I had not
been at all satisfied that violence could
serve as the positive action we must take
to save the future of our country. I fell
prey to perplexity, to a mixture of over-
lapping factors that ran the gamut of patri-
otism and religion, leniency and ruthless-
ness, faith and doubt, knowledge and the
lack of it.

Gradually I came to realize that the idea
of political assassinations that glowed once
in my imagination was beginning to dim
and lose its value as a means of bringing
about this positive action.

I remember particularly a night which
marked a turning point in the course of my
thoughts and dreams in this respect. We
had planned a course of action and decided that a certain man should cease to
exist. We studied his movements and
habits before carrying out our plan, which
was perfected in all respects. The plan
was to shoot him by night on his way
home. An execution squad was appointed

to do the shooting, covered by a second squad for protection, and a third squad for the get-away.

The appointed night came, and I went out with the attack group. Everything went according to plan.

Cries Pursued Me

As we had expected, the field was clear. The squads concealed themselves in their assigned positions, waiting for our man. As soon as he was sighted, he was met with a volley of bullets. The execution squad then withdrew, covered by the protective force, and we hurried to safety. I started the motor of my car and drove away from the scene of our carefully planned "positive action".

But suddenly there rang in my ears the sounds of screaming and wailing. I heard a woman crying, a child terrified, and a continuous, frightened call for help.

While speeding away in my car, I was overwhelmed and excited by a multitude of emotions. A strange thing was happen-

54

ing to me. The sounds were still loud in my ears: the screaming and the wailing and the crying and the frightened calls for help. I was now too far away from the scene to hear the actual sounds, but nevertheless they seemed chasing me — following me.

I arrived at my house and threw myself on my bed, my mind in agitation, my heart and conscience in unceasing turmoil. The sounds of screaming and lamentation and wailing and the calls for help continued to ring in my ears.

Thoughts in the Night

I did not sleep all night.

I remained lying on my bed in darkness, smoking continuously, trying to direct my agitated thoughts, which were no sooner collected than again distracted by the sounds that chased me.

Had I done right? I answered myself with conviction that it was for the sake of my country that I had taken this action.

Was there another way? Again I an-

swered myself, but this time in doubt.
What else *could* we have done?

But is it really possible to change the
future of our country by eliminating this
or that person? Is the problem deeper
than this?

Perplexed by the question, I answered
myself: the problem appears to be deeper.
We dream of the glory of our nation. But
which is the better way to bring it about —
to eliminate those who should be eliminat-
ed, or to bring forward those who should
be brought forward?

There on my bed I thought it through
with flashes of understanding illuminating
my reflections: yes, the important thing is
to bring forward those who can build. . . .
We dream of the glory of our nation; it is
necessary to *build* that glory.

Still tossing on my bed in a room now
full of smoke and permeated with emotions, I said to myself: And so, therefore?

I heard an internal voice asking: Therefore what?

This time I answered myself with certain conviction: I mean that our method must be changed. What we have been doing is not the positive action to which we are dedicated. The problem has roots that are deep, and is too profound to be approached in this negative way.

I felt a serene inner relief. But even so, my mental peace continued to be troubled by the sounds of screaming and wailing and crying and calling for help, striking to the depths of my heart.

Suddenly I hoped that the man would not die. It was strange to find myself at dawn wishing life for the man whom I had wished death only the previous evening!

I waited anxiously for the morning paper. The man whose assassination I had planned was out of danger. I was relieved.

The Search For An "Action"

But the main problem remained. We must find out what the positive action should be.

From that time on, our thinking was

directed to doing something more deeply rooted, more important and further reaching. Thus we began to draw the outline of the picture which materialized on the night of July 23rd: a revolution springing from the heart of the people, expressing their hopes, following the same path they had already envisioned as the great highway to freedom.

I began this new phase with the following two questions: first, what is it that we want to do? Second, what are the means to it? As I said before, the answer to the first question was to achieve freedom. But the second question — how to achieve this hope — was the point of long discussions until the very day of July 23rd.

A Single Step

Did the events of July 23rd realize all we wanted? The answer is definitely no. Those events were but the first step!

In fact, I was not diverted by the joy at our success. That joy was not enough to convince me that our hopes could now become real and that the spring of a new life had come to Egypt. I felt almost the contrary.

Every time the revolution achieved a new success, a new and heavy burden was also thrown upon my shoulders.

In Part One of what I am now writing, I said that before July 23rd I had imagined that all the nation was on the alert and ready. I thought that the nation was only waiting for a vanguard to tear down the barrier that stood in its way and would then consolidate behind that vanguard in an ordered, organized move.

I also said that I had thought that the part of vanguard was our only role, which, having been achieved in a few minutes, the ordered and organized ranks would begin to move forward.

In Part One, I also gave a picture of how dissension, chaos, vindictiveness and self-ishness were unleashed at the very first moments. Every man wanted selfishly to benefit by the revolution and attain certain individual aims.

I said, and I shall continue to say, that
that was the greatest shock of my life. But
I must admit that I should have expected
that to happen. It is impossible for hopes
to come true simply by pressing an electric
button. It is impossbile for the accumu-
lated consequences of long centuries and
successive generations to disappear in the
blink of an eye.

How Easy To Shed Blood

It was at that time easy — and it is still
easy — to shed the blood of ten, twenty or
thirty people, and thus strike fear in many
wavering hearts, thereby forcing them to
suppress their greed, vindictiveness and
selfishness. But what would have been
the result of such action?

I believe that whatever the problem is
that must be faced, the right way to effect
its solution is to trace its elements back to
their origins and by such analysis get the
true root of the matter through discovering
the causes.

It would have been unjust to institute a

rule of blood without regard for the historical circumstances through which our people have passed, and which have given us those characteristics which make us what we now are.

I have said earlier that I did not wish to claim the chair of a history professor. Nothing is further from my mind. But like an elementary student, I can only try.

Return to the Past

It fell to Egypt that she should be the geographical crossroads of the world. So often were we a channel for the invader! So often were we the prize of covetous adventurers! It is impossible to account for the many factors involved in the psychology of our people unless we carefully analyze the many circumstances that have historically beset us.

To my mind, it is not possible to disregard the Pharaonic history of Egypt, or the interaction of Greek culture and our own. Then there came the Roman invasion and the Islamic conquest, together with succeeding Arab waves of immigration.

I believe that we must also dwell at length on our history through the Middle Ages, since it was the vicissitudes of that period which contributed so much to what we think and how we act today.

If the Crusades were the beginning of the Renaissance in Europe, they were the beginning of the dark ages in our country. Our people alone bore most of the sufferings of the Crusades, out of which they emerged poor, destitute and exhausted. In their exhaustion they were simultaneously destined by circumstances to submit to and to suffer further indignity under the hoofs of the Mongol and Caucasian tyrants. They came to Egypt as slaves, murdered their masters and became masters themselves. They were driven into Egypt as Mamelukes (i.e., owned) but shortly they became kings in our good and peaceful land.

Tyranny, oppression and ruin characterized their rule in Egypt, which continued for many dark centuries. During that period, our country was transformed into

a jungle ruled by wild beasts. The Mamelukes considered it an easy prey, and they
struggled ferociously among themselves
about the sharing of the booty. The booty
was our souls, our minds, our wealth and
our land.

Residue of the Past

Sometimes when I re-read the pages of
our history, I feel a tearing grief because
of that period — a period during which we
were the victims of a tyrannous feudalism
which did nothing for us except suck the
life-blood from our veins. Nay, even worse
— it robbed us of all sense of strength and
honor. It left in the depths of our souls a
complex which we will have to fight for a
long time to overcome.

In fact, it is that complex, in my estimation, that is responsible for certain aspects in our political life. Many people,
for example, stood to one side as mere
spectators, observing our revolution, as
though they had nothing to do with it.
They only waited for the result of a strug-

gle between two opposing forces, neither of which concerned them.

Sometimes I resent this. Sometimes I demand of myself and my comrades: why don't these people come forward? Why don't they come out of their hiding places to speak up and to act? This is only to be accounted for, in my opinion, by the numbing effects of the Mameluke rule. The Mameluke rulers had fought each other, and their warriors had met in fierce battles on the streets, while the people would stampede to their houses, locking themselves in, and thus avoiding a struggle which was not their concern.

It sometimes appears to me that we content ourselves overmuch by wishful thinking. In flights of fancy we fulfill our desires and enjoy in imagination things which we never bestir ourselves to realize. Some of us are still susceptible to such daydreams. Such people have not yet fully realized that the land is actually theirs, and that they, and none other, are their own masters.

Once I tried to find out the meaning of a chant which I had so often shouted in my childhood, whenever I saw an airplane in the sky: "O, Almighty God, may disaster take the English!" (Ya 'Azeez, Ya 'Azeez. Dahiya takhud al-Ingleez). Later, I came to know that that phrase had come down to us from the days of the Mamelukes. Our forebears of that day had not used it against the English, but they used a similar one against the Turk: "O God, the Self-Revealing! Annihilate the Turk!" (Ya Rabb, Ya Mutajelle, Ahlik al-'Uthmanli) My use of it was but an adaptation of an old form to express a new feeling. The underlying constant continued the same, never changing. Only the name of the oppressor was different.

Driven by Storms

With the same unchanged spirit we used to express the same meaning, and it did not make much difference if the word "English" was substituted for the word "Turk" in accordance with the unhappy political fortunes that overtook Egypt in the interim.

And then what happened to us after the Mamelukes? The French expedition came and smashed the iron curtain which the Mongols had erected around us. New ideas flowed in, and new horizons opened up before us, of which we had been unaware.

Mohammed Ali's dynasty took over all the habits of the Mamelukes, but did attempt to clothe them in garments that were a little better suited to the nineteenth century. Thus our contact with Europe and with the whole world began anew. And thus the modern reawakening began—but it was accompanied by a new crisis.

As I see it, we were like a sick man who had been shut up in a closed room for a long time. The temperature of the closed room rose high until he was almost choked. All of a sudden a storm blew and shattered the door and windows. The currents of cold air rushed in and the perspiring sick body shivered with chill. The sick man was, to be sure, in need of a breath of air, but it was a powerful gale that blew over him. The frail and exhausted body succumbed to fever.

This was exactly what happened to our society. For us, it was a perilous experience, whereas the Europeans had evolved by an orderly process, gradually bridging the gap between the Renaissance which followed the Middle Ages and the nineteenth century. The stages of evolution there came naturally.

But with us everything came as new and strange. We had been living in isolation, cut off from the rest of the world, especially after the trade with the East had changed routes and traveled via the Cape of Good Hope. Then, suddenly we were coveted by the countries of Europe, since we became for them the bridge to be crossed for their colonies in the east and the south.

Waves of thoughts and ideas came over us while we were not yet developed enough to evaluate them. We were still living mentally in the captivity of the 13th century, in spite of a few manifestations of the nineteenth, and afterwards of the twentieth century. Our minds tried to catch up with the caravan of human progress, although we were five centuries or more behind. The pace was fearful and the journey was exhausting.

There is no doubt that this situation is responsible for the lack of a strong and united public opinion in our country. The differences between individuals are great, and between generations they are still greater.

I used to complain that the people did not know what they wanted and could not agree on any program to be followed. Then I realized that I was demanding the impossible and that I had disregarded the circumstances of our society.

We live in a society that has not yet taken form. It is still fluid and agitated and has not yet settled down or taken a stabilized shape. It is in the process of an evolution, striving to catch up with those other nations that have preceded us on the road.

With no intention of flattering, I believe that our people have nonetheless achieved a miracle. It is quite possible that any other nation, under the same conditions, would have faded away, drowned by such currents as have but submerged us. But we have stood firm against the violent flood. It is true we have almost lost our balance on certain occasions, but it is our destiny never to have fallen but that we rose again.

Sometimes I examine the conditions of an average Egyptian family among the thousands of families living in Cairo. It may be that the father is a turbaned farmer who has been born outside the city, in the heart of the countryside. The mother is a descendant of a Turkish family. The sons are being educated at an English style school, while the daughters attend schools run on the methods of the French. And all this is being backgrounded by a curious mixture of thirteenth and twentieth century ways of life.

I consider all this, and feel a deep understanding of the confusion that besets our national life and of the disorder from which we plan escape. Then I reflect: this society will develop form, consolidate and become a strong, homogeneous and unified whole. But first we must make ourselves ready to survive and make growth through the period of transition.

These are the origins of our present conditions. These are the sources from which our difficulties flow. Add to these many social and economic elements, the circumstances under which we ousted Farouk, and our natural desire to liberate our country from foreign troops—then you will realize how extensive is the scope of our necessities. Our position is blown upon by the wind from all directions. We are on a field roaring with hurricanes, dazzled by lightning and shaken by thunder. On top of all this, it would be monstrous to impose a rule of blood.

What Is The Path?

Which, then, is the right way?

What role must we undertake to achieve that way?

The way is that of political and economic freedom, and our role is that of a guardian, no more and no less. And our guardianship is only for a specified and limited time.

Our people are now like a caravan which seeks to follow a certain route, but the route is long, and the diversions to be encountered are many. Thieves and highwaymen may hold it up, and the mirage mislead it from the true way. The caravan, as a result, might be dispersed. Groups might go astray one way or the other, and individuals scatter in different directions.

This, then, is our role, the situation being what it is—to gather together the scattered and strayed parts to help them take one way, the right way. When this is done, when dangers are allayed, the caravan is left then to proceed in peace and security along the proper way.

This is our role, and I cannot conceive it to be otherwise. It would be illusion if I thought that we could solve all the problems of our country, and I do not hold with illusions. We are simply not competent to do that job, nor do we have the necessary experience.

To repeat and emphasize, our task is but to mark the way, to shepherd the strays so that they may start and remain together on the right path; to point out to those who may go off after the mirage the emptiness of their delusions.

From the start I knew that this would never be an easy task, and I realized beforehand that it would be accomplished at the expense of popularity. We had to be blunt, outspoken, armed with reason whenever we addressed the people. Our predecessors were skilled in deluding people and telling them what they liked to hear. How easy it is to appeal to people's emotions and how difficult to appeal to their reason!

We all have the same emotions—whereas our minds differ widely. The politicians of Egypt in the past were smart and capi-

talized on this fact. Their oratory left
reason severely alone, to wander aimlessly
in the wilderness. We could have done
the same. We could have smothered the
public with resounding words which were
compounded of delusion and fancy. Or
we could have inflamed them to hasty action without any planning or preparation.
We could also have left them to shout
themselves hoarse with such slogans as:
"O, God Almighty, may disaster take the
English!" just as our forefathers shouted
themselves out in the days of the Mamelukes, exhorting, "O God the Self-Revealed
—annihilate the Turk!" But nothing would
have been resolved by such sound and
fury.

But was this the mission with which
Fate had entrusted us? What would we
have really achieved if we had followed
this course?

I noted earlier, in Part One, that the
success of the Revolution depended on
the recognition by the people of the realities that faced them; it depended on its

swiftness; and now I would like to add that to maintain its success it also depends on freeing ourselves from the captivity of glittering phrases. Our revolution must be sustained by our having the courage to embark on whatever is deemed necessary, no matter what loss of popularity and applause and cheers such action may cost us. Otherwise we will have failed in our trust as leaders of the revolution.

This Is Our Role

Frequently people come to me and say: "But you are arousing certain people's resentment." To which I always reply: "The resentment of certain people is not the important factor. The real question is always: is what they resent good for the nation, or bad for themselves?"

I know that we have aroused resentment in large landowners. But was it possible not to anger them—to abandon to them the soil of our country? There were those among us who were owners of tens of thousands of acres, while others did not

74

own as much land as would be enough for
their graves.

And I know that we have angered the
politicians of the old regimes. But was it
possible not to, and simply leave them our
country, a prey to their selfishness, corruption and struggles for the fruits of author-
ity?

And I know that we have aroused the
resentment of many government officials.
But was it possible to devote more than
half of our budget to their salaries and
thus make ourselves unable to allot forty
million pounds for the productive projects
we have already undertaken? What if
we had opened the treasury—as others before us did—and given it all away to the
government employees? And after that,
what? They did not look forward to the
following year when the government
might find itself totally unable to pay their
salaries.

Nothing would have been easier than to
placate these people, and many others.
But what a price our country would have

had to pay out of its hopes and its future.

The Past and the Future

This is our role as determined for us by the history of our nation. There is no choice, no matter what the price we may have to pay. We are under no illusion concerning the task we are to achieve, or the nature of the duties imposed upon us. We removed the former king without consulting anyone because he was an obstacle in the clear way of our caravan. We began our plans for expelling the English from Egypt because their presence here weighs upon us and our progress, and leads many among us off the right track and into emotional detours.

There are the steps that had to be taken in correcting the legacy of the past. We have proceeded on the way and borne all the responsibility for everything.

But when the time came that the future of our country was to be discussed and fashioned, we said that it was no right of ours alone. To make secure the political

life of our country in the future, we sought
leaders of opinion from different classes
and beliefs. We said to them: "Draft
for the country a constitution that will
preserve things held as sacred to its people." A committee was set up to do this.

And to be sure about our economic welfare, we asked the most eminent professors in various fields of experience to create
a program to insure the prosperity and
well being of our country so that each and
every individual might be certain of his
daily bread. As a result, the Permanent
Council for the Development of National
Production was set up.

There are no limits beyond which we
will not go. Our task is the removal of
rocks and obstacles from off the way. This
is our only duty. The future and all its
challenge is work that is open to all patriots
with ideas and experience. This is a duty
and a privilege demanded of them. We
cannot perform the whole task. It is our
cherished duty, our moment of historical
responsibility, to thus bring our people at

long last together, and weld them in unity for the future—the future of Egypt—strong and free.

PART THREE

Geographical limits. A role in search of a hero. The first circle. Positive efforts in the Arab circle. Impressions on the field of battle. Imperialism and its results. Necessity of the common struggle. Numerical balance sheet of power. The interior of the dark continent. Islamic Parliament.

For a third time, I return to my thoughts on the philosophy of the revolution. I come back to it after a lapse of three months filled with swiftly developing events. During the three months I have repeatedly tried to find time in which to set down these further reflections but always the high winds of events blew upon these attempts and scattered them.

But the winds which dispersed my attempts at writing did not blow away the reflections themselves. True, they were not put upon paper, but they continued to dominate my thoughts, together with other reflections, and I constantly searched for more details, either in my memory or in daily events, in order to add them in creating a clear and correct picture.

What is this clear picture which I want to draw at this time, and what relation does it have to the attempts I have made before in the first and second parts of these reflections on the philosophy of the revolution?

In the first section, I discussed the beginning of revolution in our minds as individuals, and in our hearts as typical ex-
amples of the youth of our generation. I
also talked of revolution in the history of
our nation, and of the place of the July
23rd Revolution in that history.

In the second section, I spoke of attempts along the way to revolution, and
how the history of our people headed us
in this direction, either when we looked
back at the past—a past which is so full of
lessons—or when, in our yearning hopeful-
ness, we looked forward to the future.

Since my emphasis in the previous two
sections has been, then, on time, I therefore feel that "place" is claiming its right
to be examined. So now let me talk about
place.

It is not my intention to enter into a
complicated philosophical discussion of
time and place, but there is no doubt that
the whole universe, and not only our own
country, is conditioned by the interaction
of time and place. And when I say that in

82

our reflections on the conditions of our country we cannot forget the element of time, it is equally true we cannot forget the element of place.

In simpler terms, we cannot go back to the tenth century; we cannot wear its clothes, which appear strange and exotic to our eyes, and we cannot become lost in its thoughts, which now appear to us as layers of darkness without any ray of light.

We also cannot behave as though we were a part of Alaska, which is a part of the northernmost regions, or as if we were on Wake Island, so desolate and far away in the stretches of the Pacific.

Time, therefore, imposes its developments upon us, and place imposes on us its geographic realities.

I have tried twice to deal with the time factor. Let us try now to explore in the realm of place.

Geographical Limits

There is one thing we should agree upon

at the beginning, and before we proceed with the discussion, and that is the definition of the limits of place as far as we are concerned. If anybody tells me that place for us means this capital where we live, I differ with him. And if anyone tells me that place for us means the political boundaries of our country, I also differ.

If the whole matter were limited to our capital, or our political boundaries, it would be much simpler. We would shut ourselves in, and live in an ivory tower, and we would try to our utmost to get away from the world, its problems, wars and crises, which all burst in on us through the doors of our country and influence us, though we have nothing to do with them.

The age of isolation is gone.

And gone are the days in which barbed wire served as demarcation lines, separating and isolating countries from one another. No country can escape looking beyond its boundaries to find the source of the currents which influence it, how it can live with others, how . . . and how. . . .

And no state can escape trying to determine its status within its living space and trying to see what it can do in that space, and what is its field of activities and its positive role in this troubled world.

Sometimes I sit in my study reflecting on the subject, asking myself: What is our positive role in this troubled world, and where is the place in which we should fulfill that role?

I review our circumstances and discover a number of circles within which our activities inescapably must be confined and in which we must try to move.

Fate does not jest and events are not a matter of chance—there is no existence out of nothing. We cannot look at the map of the world without seeing our own place upon it, and that our role is dictated by that place.

Can we fail to see that there is an Arab circle surrounding us—that this circle is a part of us, and we are a part of it, our history being inextricably part of its history.

These are facts and no mere idle talk. Can we possibly ignore the fact that there is an African continent which Fate decreed us to be a part of, and that it is also decreed that a terrible struggle exists for its future —a sruggle whose results will be either for us or against us, with or without our will? Can we further ignore, the existence of an Islamic world, with which we are united by bonds created not only by religious belief, but also reinforced by historic realities? As I have said once, Fate is no jester.

It is not without significance that our country is situated west of Asia, in contiguity with the Arab states with whose existence our own is interwoven. It is not without significance, too, that our country lies in northeast Africa, overlooking the Dark Continent, wherein rages a most tumultous struggle between white colonizers and black inhabitants for control of its unlimited resources. Nor is it without significance that, when the Mongols swept away the ancient capitals of Islam,

Islamic civilization and the Islamic heritage fell back on Egypt and took shelter there. Egypt protected them and saved them, while checking the onslaught of the Mongols at 'Ain Jalut. All these are fundamental realities with deep roots in our lives which we cannot—even if we try—escape or forget.

A Role in Search of a Hero

I do not know why I recall, whever I reach this point in my recollections as I meditate alone in my room, a famous tale by a great Italian poet, Luigi Pirandello—"Six Characters in Search of an Author." The pages of history are full of heroes who created for themselves roles of glorious valor which they played at decisive moments. Likewise the pages of history are also full of heroic and glorious roles which never found heroes to perform them. For some reason it seems to me that within the Arab circle there is a role, wandering aimlessly in search of a hero. And I do not know why it seems to me that this role, exhausted by its wanderings, has at last settled down, tired and weary, near the borders of our country and is beckoning to us to move, to take up its lines, to put on its costume, since no one else is qualified to play it.

Here, let me hasten to say that this role is not one of leadership. It is rather a role of interaction with, and responsibility to all the above-mentioned factors. It is a role such as to spark this tremendous power latent in the area surrounding us; a role tantamount to an experiment, with the aim of creating a great strength which will then undertake a positive part in the building of the future of mankind.

The First Circle

There can be no doubt that the Arab circle is the most important, and the one with which we are most closely linked. For its peoples are intertwined with us by history. We have suffered together, we have gone through the same crises, and when we fell beneath the hooves of

the invaders' steeds, they were with us under the same hooves.

We are also bound in this circle by a
common religion.

The center of Islamic learning has always moved within the orbit of its several
capital cities—first Mecca, then shifting to
Kufa, then to Damascus, next to Baghdad,
and finally to Cairo.

Lastly, the fact that the Arab states are
contiguous has joined them together in a
geographical framework made solid by
all these historical, material and spiritual
factors.

So far as I can recall, the first glimmers
of Arab awareness began to steal into my
consciousness when I was a student in
secondary school. I used to go out on a
general strike with my comrades every
year on the second of December to protest
the Balfour Declaration which Britain had
made on behalf of the Jews, giving them
a national home in Palestine, thus tyran-
nously wresting it from its rightful owners.
And at that time, when I asked myself

why I went out on strike with such zeal, and why I was angry about this act by a country I had never seen, I could find no answer except in the echoes of sympathetic emotion.

Then a kind of understanding began to develop when I became a student in the Military Academy, where I studied in particular the history of all past military campaigns in Palestine and in general the history of the area and its conditions which have made of it during the past hundred years an easy prey for the fangs of hungry beasts. Things grew still clearer and the underlying realities became apparent when, in the General Staff College I began to study the late Palestine campaign and the problems of the Mediterranean in detail.

The result was that when the Palestine crisis began, I was utterly convinced that the fighting there was not taking place on foreign soil, nor was our part in it a matter of sentiment. It was a duty necessitated by self-defense.

Positive Efforts in the Arab Circle

I remember that just after the announcement of the decision to partition Palestine in September 1947, the Free Officers held a meeting and decided to help in the resistance. Next day I knocked on the door of Hajj Amin al Husseini, Mufti of Palestine, who was then living in Zaitoun. I said to him, "You have need of officers to lead in the struggle and to train volunteers. In the Egyptian Army there is a large number of officers who wish to offer their services. They are at your command any time you wish."

He said that he was pleased with this spirit, but that he thought the permission of the Egyptian Government would be necessary. Then he said, "I will give you my answer after asking permission." A few days later I went back and he told me that the Government's reply had been negative.

However, we did not let this stop us.

Some time later, the artillery of Ahmad Abdul Aziz began to bombard the Jewish

colonizers south of Jerusalem. The com-
manding officer of the artillery was Kemal ed-Din Hussein, a member of the Con-
stituent Committee of the Free Officers,
which has since become the Council of
the Revolution.

I remember another secret of that time
—the best secret of all. Hassan Ibrahim
had gone to Damascus to meet with some
of the officers of Fauzi al-Qawuqji, who
was leader of the Arab Liberation Forces,
and who was preparing for a decisive battle in northern Palestine. Hassan Ibrahim
and Abdul Latif Baghdadi drew up a bold
plan to strike a successful blow in this
battle. The main feature of the plan took
account of the fact that the Liberation
Forces had no air support to give them the
advantage: attack from the air might indeed be the decisive factor in the battle.
But where could the Liberation Forces
get the aircraft to implement this attack?

Hassan Ibrahim and Abdul Latif Bag-
hadi did not hesitate. They decided that
the Egyptian Air Force should fulfill this

mission. But how? Egypt had not yet
entered the war in Palestine. And the
armed forces, including the Air Force,
were kept under strict surveillance. Nevertheless they did not give in to despair.

There had been a strange activity on the
military airfields. Planes began to be re-
paired and prepared; the infection of these
obvious efforts traveled like a fever among
the pilots. But only a few knew the secret,
knew that planes and pilots were making
ready for the day when a secret signal
should come from Syria, whereupon they
would take off to engage with all their
strength in the decisive battle over the
Holy Land. Then they would proceed to
the airfield near Damascus, land, wait for
reaction in Egypt, and then decide what
to do next. It seemed likely that every
pilot participating in this action would be
court martialed; I remember that many
of them had put their affairs in order in
case circumstances should prevent their
return for some years.

In planning this bold enterprise, the

underlying motive of the Executive Committee of the Free Officers—and certainly the same idea inspired all the pilots participating in the plan—was not simply a love of adventure, or only fellow-feeling for the Palestinian Arabs. It was rather the clear awareness that Rafah was not the real outer boundary of our country, and that our own security required the defense of the boundaries of the sister Arab states among whom we were placed by Fate.

Impressions on the Field of Battle

The plan was not carried out because we never received the secret signal from Syria. And afterwards, circumstances brought about the official entry of the Arab armies into Palestine.

For the present, I do not wish to dwell upon the details of that war. It is a subject about which accounts differ. What concerns me is the important lesson it teaches.

The Arabs entered Palestine in a single

94

wave of enthusiasm. They did so on the
basis of common knowledge and a common estimate shared by all as to the outer
borders of their security. The Arab states
emerged from Palestine with a common
bitterness and disappointment; then, each
in its own internal affairs encountered the
same factors, the same ruling forces that
had brought about their defeat, and forced
them to bow their heads in humiliation
and shame.

I thought about these things a good
deal while alone in the trenches and foxholes of the Menshia hills. I was then
with General Staff, Sixth Battalion, which
was stationed in that sector, sometimes
defending it, more often moving to the
attack. I used to go out among the ruins
left by enemy artillery fire and there let
my imagination soar.

Sometimes I would be carried high up
to the region of the stars; from this lofty
height I would gaze down in my mind's
eye over the whole region. And the picture began to be more distinct.

Down there below is where we are dug
in and surrounded; here is the position of
our battalion, and there are the other bat-
talions with us in the line. Beyond are
the forces of the enemy surrounding us;
and beyond them, more of our forces, who
are in turn encircled, though less restricted
in movement.

We were sorely pressed, but the political climate in the capital, whence we received our orders, created a siege there—a
tighter and more crippling siege than anything we experienced while dug in at the
Faluja pocket.

Then, over there, are the forces of our
brothers-at-arms, our brother Arabs, brothers in the common enterprise and in the
common urge that hastened us all to the
land of Palestine. There are the armies
of our brothers, army after army, each one
surrounded by those same circumstances
which have also throttled their governments.

They all, armies and governments,
seemed to be pawns, devoid of power and

self-motivation, moved only by the hands of players. And behind the lines, all our peoples seemed to be the victims of a well-knit conspiracy which deliberately suppressed the realities of what was happening, the facts of the actual situation.

And then I would come down to earth again, and feel that what I was doing was to defend my home and children, nothing more; that my fanciful dreams—Arab capitals, nations, peoples, history—all this meant nothing. This was when, wandering among the ruins, I would come across refugee children looking for shelter, having fallen into the clutches of the siege following the destruction of their homes and the loss of their possessions. I remember one small girl who was about my own daughter's age. I saw her just as she had wandered into a zone of danger and whistling bullets, driven by the lash of hunger and cold to search for a bit of food or a piece of cloth. And I said to myself: This could happen to my little girl.

For I was certain that what was hap-

pening in Palestine could happen to any
one of the Arab states so long as it remained subject to the factors and forces
that governed it at that time.

Imperialism and Its Results

When the struggle was over in Palestine
and the siege lifted, and I had returned to
Egypt, the Arab circle in my eyes had become a single entity. The events that
have taken place since have confirmed my
belief. I have followed developments in
the Arab countries, and I find they match,
point for point. What happened in Cairo
had its counterpart in Damascus the next
day, and in Beirut, in Amman, in Baghdad
and elsewhere. This all fitted in with the
picture drawn by long experience. It is
a single region. The same circumstances,
the same factors, even the same forces,
united against all of it.

And it was clear that the foremost of
these forces was imperialism.

Even Israel itself is but a result of imperialism. For if Palestine had not fallen

under the British mandate, Zionism would
never had been able to muster enough support to realize a national home in Palestine. The idea would have remained a
mad hopeless dream.

As I set down these reflections, I have
before me the memoirs of Chaim Weizmann, first President of the Republic of
Israel and its real founder. They are published in his well known book *Trial and
Error*. There are certain passages that are
most revealing. For example, he says:

"It was necessary that a great nation
support us, and there were in the world
two nations, either of which could do so:
Germany or Great Britain. As for Germany, it had already decided to stay aloof.
But Britain had surrounded us with care
and sympathy."

And then this statement struck me:

"During the Sixth Zionist Congress
which we convened in Switzerland, Herzl's
stand made it clear to world Jewry that
Great Britain, and Great Britain alone, to
the exclusion of all other nations, recog-

nized the Jews as a nation having a distinct
and independent existence. We Jews de-
serve to have a fatherland and a state:
Herzl proceeded to read a letter from Lord
Latterson on behalf of the British Government which proved the point, and which
offered Uganda as a national home.

"The members of the Congress decided
to accept this offer, but afterwards we
stifled it in the cradle and quietly buried
it. After this episode, Great Britain turned
around and offered us the region around
al-Arish in Sinai: Britain was eager to
please us. As a result of this offer, we
formed a large commission of Jewish
scholars who traveled to Egypt to study
the area. They were received in Cairo by
Lord Cromer, the British High Commis-
sioner, with a show of every concern for
our aspirations for a national home. The
commission, however, did not consider the
region to be one which would satisfy the
objectives we sought in a national home.

"Later, I met Lord Balfour, Foreign
Minister of Great Britain, who began im-

mediately to ask questions. 'Why didn't
you agree to establish the national home in
Uganda?' I replied, 'Zionism is a national-
istic, political movement, it is true. However, we cannot neglect the spiritual side
of it. I am absolutely certain if we neglect
the spiritual side, we shall never be able
to realize the nationalist political dream.'
Then I said, 'What would you say if someone said to you: Take Paris in exchange
for London. Would you do it?' "

Again, this passage caught my eye:

"I returned to London in the fall of 1921
with the objective of supervising the writing of the draft terms of the British mandate in Palestine. It was necessary that
this document be presented to the League
of Nations for final approval, the mandate
having been previously confirmed in prin-
ciple at the San Remo Conference.

"Lord Curzon had taken over the Foreign Office from Lord Balfour and was responsible for the draft proposal. In London with me was the famous jurist Ben
Cohen, one of the most able legal drafts-

men in the world; and Eric Forbes-Adam,
Curzon's secretary, cooperated with us.

"Between us and Curzon there were differences from start to finish. We wrote
for the draft preamble a phrase by which
we wanted to bind Britain to the promise
of Lord Balfour and insure that its policy
in Palestine should be based on the prin-
ciple of the Jewish national home. The
text we wanted was: 'Recognizing the historic rights of the Jews in Palestine,' but
Curzon said that he preferred to soften the
phrase so the Arabs should not be made
angry in reading it, and that he thought it
should read: 'Recognizing the historical
connection of the Jews in Palestine.' "

I would like to go on at length quoting
from Weizmann's book, but we all know
that these bygone events were the germs
of the terrible complications which rent
Palestine and finally destroyed its existence.

Necessity of the Common Struggle

Let me go back, now, to what I was say-

ing — that imperialism is the great force
that is imposing a murderous, invisible
siege upon the whole region, a siege one
hundred times more powerful and pitiless
than that which was laid upon us in our
trenches at Faluja, or that which encircled
our individual armies and our capitals
whence we received our orders.

When all these truths had impressed
themselves upon me, I began to realize
the need for a common struggle. I said
to myself that so long as the region is one
region, sharing the same conditions and
problems, and the same future (and, however he tries to change his disguise, the
same enemy) — so long as this is true, why
do we scatter our efforts?

The experiences which followed the July
23rd revolution have increased my conviction of the necessity for a common struggle. And now, the hidden parts of the long
developing picture began to be disclosed,
the obscuring shadows began to disappear.

I admit that in the process, I also began
to see the great obstacles which block the

path to the common struggle, but I began
to believe that these obstacles, being the
creation of the common enemy, had to be
removed.

Finally, I began to make poltical contacts for the sake of unifying the struggle
by whatever means. After a month of
such contacts, I came to the important con-
clusion that the first obstacle in our path is
doubt. It was clear that the roots of this
doubt were planted in us by our old common enemy in order to prevent us from em-
barking upon unified action.

I recall sitting recently talking with the
brother of an Arab politician. One of his
colleagues was with us. I led the conversation; his part was to reply to my questions. He would say something and then
turn around to his colleague to gauge the
effect of what he was saying, instead of
gauging its effect upon me. I said to him:
"Overcome your doubts. Say what you
think. Look me in the eye instead of turning your face away."

I do not want to minimize the obstacles

to unity in the common struggle. There is no doubt that these obstacles have their roots in the nature of the situation and in the historical and geographical circumstances of our people. But it is also certain that with a little flexibility, based on foresight, not on neglect, it will be possible to call into being a plan upon which everyone will be able to agree without reservation— a plan for carrying out the common struggle.

I do not doubt for a moment that our common effort will achieve for us and our peoples everything we desire. For I shall always maintain that we are strong. The only trouble is that we do not realize just how strong we are.

Numerical Balance of Power

We make the wrong definition of strength. It is not strength to shout at the top of the lungs: real strength lies in acting positively with all the effective means at our command. When I try to analyze the elements of our strength, there are three main sources which should first be taken into account.

The first of these sources is that we are a community of neighboring peoples linked by all the material and moral ties possible, and that we have characteristics and abilities and a civilization which have given rise to three holy religions — factors which cannot be ignored in the effort to build a secure and peaceful world. So much for the first source.

As for the second source of strength, it is our land itself and its position on the map — that important, strategic position which embraces the crossroads of the world, the thoroughfare of its traders and the passageway of its armies.

There remains the third source: oil — a sinew of material civilization without which all its machines would cease to function. The great factories, producing every kind of goods; all the instruments of land, sea and air communication; all the weapons of war, from the mechanical bird above the clouds to the submarine beneath the waves — without oil, all would turn back to naked metal, covered with rust, incapable of motion or use.

Here I would like to pause for a moment to deal with the subject of oil. Perhaps its existence as a material necessity which has been established by facts and figures will afford a useful model for our analysis of the importance of the sources of strength in our country.

I read recently an article published by the University of Chicago on the world oil situation. It would be a good thing if every Arab could read it, grasp its implication, and see the great significance revealed by its statistics.

The article points out, for example, that in the Arab countries the effort to extract oil requires comparatively little capital. Oil companies spent 60 million dollars in Colombia, beginning in 1916, and did not discover a drop of oil until 1936. They spent $44 million in Venezuela, and did not get a drop of oil for 15 years. They spent $39 million in the Dutch Indies before they struck oil. According to the article, it all adds up to the fact that the cost of producing a barrel of oil in North America is 78 cents, in South America, 48 cents, but in the Arab countries the cost is only 10 cents.

The article further says that the center of world oil production has shifted from the United States, where oil wells are going dry, where the cost of land is going up and the wages of workers have risen, to the Arab area, where the fields are still virgin, where vast tracts of land continue to cost almost nothing, and where labor is comparatively cheap. Half the proved reserves of oil in the world lie beneath Arab soil, the remainder being divided among the United States, Russia, the Caribbean area and other sections of the globe.

It is a fact, too, that the average daily production per well is 11 barrels in the United States, 230 barrels in Venezuela, and 4,000 barrels in the Arab area. Have I made clear how great is the importance of this element of strength? I hope so.

Se we are strong. Strong not in the loudness of our voices when we wail or shout for help, but rather when we remain silent and measure the extent of our ability to act; when we really understand the strength resulting from the ties binding us together, making our land a single region from which no part can withdraw, and of which no part, like an isolated island, can be defended without defense of the whole.

The Interior of the Dark Continent

So much for the first circle in which we must turn, and in which we must act with all our ability — the Arab circle.

If we consider next the second circle — the continent of Africa — I may say without exaggeration that we cannot, under any circumstances, however much we might desire it, remain aloof from the terrible and sanguinary conflict going on there today between five million whites and 200 million Africans. We cannot do so for an important and obvious reason: we are *in* Africa. The peoples of Africa will con-

tinue to look to us, who guard their northern gate, and who constitute their link with
the outside world. We will never in any
circumstances be able to relinquish our responsibility to support, with all our might,
the spread of enlightenment and civilization to the remotest depths of the jungle.

There remains another important reason.
It is that the Nile is the life artery of our
country, bringing water from the heart of
the continent.

As a final reason, the boundaries of our
beloved brother, the Sudan, extend far into
the depths of Afrcia, bringing into contiguity the politically sensitive regions in
that area.

The Dark Continent is now the scene of
a strange and excited turbulence: the white
man, representing various European nations, is again trying to re-divide the map
of Africa. We shall not, in any circum-
stance, be able to stand idly by in the face
of what is going on, in the false belief that
it will not affect or concern us.

I will continue to dream of the day when

I will find in Cairo a great African institute dedicated to unveiling to our view the dark reaches of the continent, to creating in our minds an enlightened African consciousness, and to sharing with others from all over the world the work of advancing the welfare of the peoples of this continent.

Islamic Parliament

There remains the third circle, which circumscribes continents and oceans, and which is the domain of our brothers in faith, who, wherever under the sun they may be, turn as we do, in the direction of Mecca, and whose devout lips speak the same prayers.

When I went with the Egyptian delegation to the Kingdom of Sa'udi Arabia to offer condolences on the death of its great sovereign, my belief in the possibility of extending the effectiveness of the Pilgrimage, building upon the strength of the Islamic tie that binds all Muslims, grew very strong. I stood before the Ka'ba, and in my mind's eye I saw all the regions of

111

the world which Islam has reached. Then
I found myself saying that our view of the
Pilgrimage must change. It should not be
regarded as only a ticket of admission into
Paradise after a long life, or as a means of
buying forgiveness after a merry one. It
should become an institution of great
political power and significance. Journal-
ists of the world should hasten to cover the
Pilgrimage, not because it is a traditional
ritual affording interesting reports for the
reading public, but because of its function
as a periodic political conference in which
the envoys of the Islamic states, their leaders of thought, their men learned in every
branch of knowledge, their writers, their
captains of industry, their merchants and
their youth can meet, in order to lay down
in this Islamic-world-parliament the broad
lines of their national policies and their
pledges of mutual cooperation from one
year to another.

Pious and humble, but strong, they
should assemble, stripped of greed, but
active; weak before God, but mighty

against their problems and their enemies; longing for an afterlife, but convinced of their place in the sun, a place they must fill in this existence.

I remember that I mentioned some of these thoughts to His Majesty, King Sa'ud, and he said to me, "It is indeed the real *raison d'etre* of the Pilgrimage." To tell the truth, I myself am unable to imagine any other *raison d'etre*.

When I consider the 80 million Muslims in Indonesia, and the 50 million in China, and the millions in Malaya, Siam and Burma, and the nearly 100 million in Pakistan, and the more than 100 million in the Middle East, and the 40 million in the Soviet Union, together with the other millions in far-flung parts of the world — when I consider these hundreds of millions united by a single creed, I emerge with a sense of the tremendous possibilities which we might realize through the cooperation of all these Muslims, a cooperation going not beyond the bounds of their natural loyalty to their own countries, but nonetheless enabling them and their brothers in faith to wield power wisely and without limit.

And now I go back to that wandering mission in search of a hero to play it. Here is the role. Here are the lines, and here is the stage. We alone, by virtue of our place, can perform the role.

NOTES ABOUT THE AUTHOR

Gamal Abdul Nasser was born in Beni Mor, a small town in Asiut Province, Upper Egypt, on January 15, 1918, the son of a good middle class family. At the age of eight, he was sent by his father to be educated in Cairo, where he was so taken by the beauty of the city that he often expressed his feelings in his letters to his parents.

In the same year, his mother, to whom he was strongly attached, died. Her loss deeply affected him and tended to increase his natural propensity for privacy and contemplation.

In 1934, his father and three brothers joined him in Cairo. He obtained his Secondary School Certificate with distinction from Al Nahda Al Misria School. He displayed an interest in law and the history of great men.

He entered the Military College in 1937. At that time the number of students was less than ninety, but it had begun to increase steadily after the 1936 Anglo-Egyptian Treaty. As a student, young Nasser was noted for his exemplary conduct, his self-reliance and his serious outlook.

Likewise, he was known for his outspokenness
and his rebellion against colonialism. He was
possessed of a strong, attractive personality which
commanded the respect and affection of his fellow students, who looked to him for leadership.
He was extremely modest, with a developed sense
of self-respect. He was a young man of few
words, but once he made up his mind, it was
difficult to persuade him to change it. Nevertheless, he was always open to conviction by the
truth. He never embarked on any action without careful planning and study. In fact, his whole
personality is reflected clearly in his book.

On graduating from the Military College, he
joined the Third Rifle Brigade and was transferred to Mankbad in Asiut, where he met Anwar
Al Sadat, Zakaria Mohie El Din (now members
of the Revolution Command Council) and Ahmed Anwar (now Chief of the Military Police).

In 1939, he was sent to Alexandria, where he
met Abdul Hakim Amer, now a member of the
Revolution Command Council, who had been
graduated from the Military College a year after
Nasser. In 1942, he was transferred to Al Ala-
mein, and later to Alexandria, where he followed

at close quarter the political tension which en-
gulfed Egypt at that time.

He served as a Lieutenant with the Fifth In-
fantry Brigade, but could not tolerate the conditions then obtaining in the Army, which he could
observe but was powerless to correct, so he asked
to be transferred to the Sudan. There he was
joined by Abdul Hakim Amer, and the two served
together in Jabal El Awlia. Despite their isolation, they were happy and soon became fast
friends, sharing the same views on Egypt and on
putting an end to the corruption rife in the ad-
ministration.

In 1942, he was also appointed a teacher at the
Military College. Later, he entered the Army
Staff College, graduating with honor. During his
studies at the latter, he met other colleagues, and
as a result of their studies of how to protect Cairo
and its approaches from ground and air enemy
forces, they were enabled to put this information
to good use when they staged their coup d'etat.

Colonel Nasser is married, and has two daughters, Huda and Mona, and three sons, Khaled,
Abdul Hamid, and Hakim Amer.

Before the outbreak of the Palestine war, he

tendered his resignation from the Army to fight as a volunteer, despite the fact that he was the sole support of his family, but his resignation was rejected. The tragedies and scandals he witnessed during his action in the Palestine war filled him with wrath against the responsible authorities, especially when he realized the Army's dire need for munitions and arms which were withheld from it. He was further incensed by the episode of Al Majdal, which the Army was ordered by Farouk to capture, although it was not in a position to undertake this task.

His heroism in the Palestine war is attested to by all those who fought with him; he always led his men in action, and was shot above the heart in one of the battles. He was taken to a hospital where he was expected to recover in one month, but escaped after a few days to return to Palestine. There he took part in the Faluja battle, which added further honors to his military career.

There in Palestine he met the rest of his colleagues of the present Revolution Command Council. He hand-picked each with meticulous care and having satisfied himself as to their loyalty he began to plan with them their next move, and to gather information through loyal sources in the Army, the Palace and the Cabinet. Finally they were able to stage, on July 23, 1952, the movement which saved the country from the clutches of reaction with its attendant corruption, and launched it on the road of justice, progress and stability. (Prepared by the Egyptian Embassy, Washington, D. C., 1954.)

Date Due

APR 10 '59			
OCT 13 '61			
	PRINTED	IN U. S. A.	